MÍCHEÁL FANNING

Verbum et Verbum

SALMON POETRY

Published in 1997 by
Salmon Publishing Ltd,
Cliffs of Moher, Co. Clare

A catalogue record for this book is available from the British Library.

Salmon Publishing gratefully acknowledges the
financial assistance of the Arts Council.

ISBN 1 897648 89 8

Cover artwork by Brenda Friel
Cover design by Brenda Dermody of Estresso
Set by Siobhán Hutson
Printed by Betaprint, Clonshaugh, Dublin 17

For Nóirín O Farrell Fanning,
Peadar, Ruth, Rachel

Acknowledgements

Versions of these poems appeared previously in the following publications: *The Salmon; Honest Ulsterman; The Big Spoon; Acumen; Journal of Irish Colleges of Physicians and Surgeons; Journal of the Irish Dental Association; Staple; Optimism; Envoi.*

Grateful thanks to: *Coiscéim* for 'Adamh agus Ádhamh' from *An Solas Geal Lonrach* (Coiscéim, 1992); and Pádraig Ó Snodaigh for his poem 'Ó Pharnell go Queenie'.

The following texts were enlightening sources: *The Book of Kells* with A Study by Françoise Henry (Thames and Hudson, 1974); *The Book of Kells* by Peter Brown (Thames and Hudson, 1980); *The Book of Kells* by Bernard Meehan (Thames and Hudson, 1994); *The Book of Kells* (Studio Editions, London 1992). For background information on 5th, 6th, 7th and 8th century Christianity I have resourced essays by Tomás Cardinal O Fiach and Kathleen Hughes from *The Course of Irish History*, edited by TW Moody and FX Martin (Mercier Press, 1984). *The Annals of Ireland* by the Four Masters, De Burca, Dublin 1990 has provided a backdrop of information on the 7th, 8th and 9th centuries.

By the Same Author

The Love Letters of Daniel O Connell (Inné, 1992, and Institute of Public Administration for D.O.C.A.L. in *People Power*, edited by Maurice R. O Connell, Dublin 1993); *Tombolo* (Lapwing Publications, Belfast 1995); *An Solas Geal Lonrach* (Coiscéim, 1992); *Déithe An tSolais* (Coiscéim, 1994).

Contents

I

Pád's Crib

for my brothers and my sister

Pádraig constructed the pyramidal
crib with alder twigs

to capture lusty, speckled
thrushes in the snow.

The six timid children
from ten down waited

behind the screen curtain
in the holly adorned kitchen.

The eldest, Pád, yanked the twine
to incarcerate the captive.

We settled for a blackbird
Anno Nivis Magnae:

The Year of the High Snows
and Blissful Blanket Blizzards.

The Culpable Captors
liberated her, whom they feared.

She flew off amongst
The Snow Sky Pines.

Lasting Light
(Cahir I)

Lasting light
illuminates the halcyon river
and Cahir bridge.

A kingfisher dips low
and swift, blue flash
down the turn of stream.

Cahir river's
pools and ponds
suffuse.

The river ripples
through the marshy fields
where curlew whistle-whines.

Solitary egret, brilliant white,
walks. Runs. Calls imperiously
across the stream.

Cahir II

Day surrenders
to interminable
evening
in Cahir.

The river drawls,
proceeds in its own time.
Pebble popped in a pool
begets a ripple rhyme.

The children ring-a-rosy
round Cahir's fields.

The white-headed cattle laze
into the wash. Car lights
advent. Seagulls whimper
in cinereous light.

The splashing ocean
drowned in chromatics
of day and night –
blazing mix.

Christmas Morning (1971)

I
My father rose out
first to prepare the oven,
then my mother
in her long blue night-gown

placed the white plucked turkey
in the Stanley oven.
I walked for the can
of milk to O'Donnell's.

Five cats scampered
round the steel buckets
outside in the back-yard of the
three-storey yellow house.

II
Groups of two and three visit
each other. The whitewashed
wall circumcircles the village
this Christ's season.

From Nóra's I hear
the drum of sea;
waves rumble
on the shell song shore.

The raucous swell
rolls
as I clog down
Strand Road.

The clamourous ocean
resounds on the strand,
sapphire sea is incarnate,
chameleon.

I dash on by the ivory spray,
animated with a hailshower
that commences,
quickly ceases.

It's timely to return
to the village among the maroon
maple trees
where families feast.

Rún

for Tom Walsh

Friends join me
in my west coast retreat.
Lights from the villages
candle our walk,

beacon from the ports
of Tralee, Fenit
Ballyheigue to Maharees,
Castle and Derrymore.

I have overheard the fishermen collogue
as they shoot lobster pots, miles from Muchaloch;
other times, haul nets from pelagic,
summer waters, ten knots from here.

I am the demure fisherman,
born of the sea ;
Survivor of a green ship
I am loveless and disaffected.

I quit all that I have known.
I'll map
across the cerulean sea
for five and twenty years.

When confidence is conferred,
I shall gybe from any world port,
to concourse with you, friends,
on our social shores.

II

Demiurge

for J.P. Murray

A sanguine farmer
yomps boggy land
to construct
the stone ditch boundary,
up beyond.

Agricola venti rarely meets
another Soul,
here, on the nocturnal mountain.

The Maker arranges nouns,
verbs, adjectives, the infinitive
and metaphors
And places appropriate stones
dexterously to structure
the storm strafed wall.

St. Francis De Sales – Patron Saint of Authors

Intercede for the salvation
of all authors.

Protect us
from cacology.

Introduce us to the devout
Life of the Author, Adonai.

Instruct us in the discovery
of our Secret Language.

Lead us not
into logomachy.

Deliver us from the propensity
towards hyperbole.

Let us forgive those
who criticise us much.

Sylleptic saint sing us
a treatise on the love of God:

'God is
the Word

*et le Verbe était Dieu
et il a habité parmi nous.'*

Etymological Saint of Nouns
pray for us at the hour of our bathos.

Console us and help us to laugh
at our malapropisms.

French Ferry Frigate

for Rachel

In a cabin,
she listens to the unctuous
seawater,
lashing steel skin.

Later in a room without a porthole,
she sinks into deep sleep,
up and down,
the sea reaching her
unconscious.

The ship bursts a path,
cranking on the ocean.

Outside on the beaches of
Utah,
Omaha,
Gold,
Juno,
Sword,

'*La princesse Perdue*',
surfaces a phoenix,
one hundred and fifteen
concrete caissons
deployed fifty years ago.

Six hundred million
years of age,
the sandstone cliffs
of France.

She finds a ladybird
on deck,
and races along corridors
and stairs,
gazes at four hundred
passengers.

In midship,
three German card players
shuffle
and deal trumpcards.

In a cabin
with a mirror
the size of a man
her father is phlegmatic,
he with his many defences,
she with none.

The ship is delayed against
the running tide,
a furling storm wanes.
Life respires.

Red Cross trucks bring supplies
to former Yugoslavia.
Now more than ever
we manufacture weapons,
more deadly weapons of mass
destruction,
'deterrent' a tragic irony?
Not an obloquy, but a truth;
thirteen-year-olds run amok
in Monrovia and Mogadishu.

She trips along,
her ladybird lost
in the assembly station,
bridge deck,
where a safety notice reads –
'*Au signal d'alarme* –
composé de sept coups courts,
… *et d'un long coup* –,
procéde au point
'*Point de Rassamblement C.'*

On the horizon, Phoebus and Phoebe,
vis à vis,
fishing boats,
cargo ships with containers
from China and Japan
appear and disappear.
Pleasure boats temerarious approach
for minutes, almost meet
then depart for eternity.
We pray for our safe passage.

Carnac

for Mícheál O Coileáin

Eight lines of Gallic Stones,
two miles long: Theopathy.

Seventy tonne stones hauled here
by resolute Hunters and Gatherers
of Carnac, for this Vulcan monument:
Sun Temple or Dolmen Theocracy.

Vibrant children play
Round and round roborant Stone Circles,
Along theomorphic lines of
Tribe Fathers and Mothers: Theogony.

Immanent Stonelines of Solstice,
Immolation and Theomania.

Two thousand Doleritic Stones
of Carnac: Theophany.

Venezia

I

Mendelssohn paused,
Music on water.

Taxis, waterbus and steamboats
chug staccato.

Mozart halted at the Ferrovia,
to rest at a canal intersection.

Vivaldi in the throes of offertory
succumbed to symphony.

Wagner scored aria, oratorio
and the Grand Finale.

Piazza San Marco played host
to string quartet '*Glorio a Dio*'.

The Doge's Palace marked for brass,
base drum and cymbal concerto.

II

They race the course up and down the Gala canal:
Puparrini, Mascarete, Caorline and Gondolini:

gondolas of different shape,
size and colour.

Gianni, Umberto, Mario, Giovanni, Luciano,
and Giuseppe, stroke in rhythm:

Gondoliers in their colours: Bianco,
Viola, Rosa, Verde, Marrone and Rosso,

The battles of *La Regata* Storica
on the Water Streets commence,

Boatmen and Boatwomen unfurl water
stretch on their oar for home.

III
Byron and Hemmingway
bestrode the Bellissima.

Dickens and George Elliot
conflated with the Serenissima.

Goethe nodded in recognition of her glory,
Nietzsche succumbed to her Art and Pride.

Pound excogitated:
urbem felicem laudo

and passed down the cathartic water city
in black-draped gondola to the immortal coast.

Shelley in a pall of darkness accompanied
Clara's cortege to Lido's Home.

Othello and Desdemona –
exhumed, garrulous, gay ghosts.

IV
Monet, Manet, Renoir
reflect the circumfluous city;

the subconscious compact
municipality of Titian.

Pallas restrained Mars,
Tintoretto proposed.

Triumphal King and Queens
ride the water streets.

Gondolas fly across
the sky of Venezia.

Carlo Finotello rowed the canal
to his parking canopy set on poles.

V
Venezia, here we shelter
from dispassion and relinquish alarm.

We purchase Venetian scenes at fifty
thousand lira to ferry Venice home.

III

The Meeting

So I met you, our fingers touched
to fondle each other.

The picture – three bronzed girls
looking to the scarlet Horizon –
hung in the Rathgar apartment.
I was made feel at home.
Your laugh was as gay as Youth.
You wore long sea-green dresses
in the middle of a biting
Dublin winter.

I was in conflict
and dissociated.
You left me for what you thought
was everything.
I shall depart from you
as the presageful dream said
I may do.

Morriston

for Nóirín

She sleeps in the front room,
where the furniture is coated in marble
from a village mine
in the mountains of Italy.
She sleeps while the moon is still,
increscent, a cradle in the sky.
The lone bird intones morn,
the trees' black silhouettes fill the street.
He awakes beside her, she sleeps.
The rose buds expose in the garden,
sunlight radiant.

Morning dream: they laugh
on the basalt cliffs.
He picks tulips for her. 'Thanks'.
Mother-God tiptoes lightly the field,
Cleopatras flap wings, jovial flight,
towards rugose sea.

They journey on, two pristine souls,
soul to soul.
They provide each other new life as well,
the confident trip
through Morriston fields.
He slips back
to join her in conjugal
sleep.

Canto of Self-Doubt

for Kitty and James Brosnan

Our son plays the Solfeggietto trill
burst of semiquavers on the piano
by C.P.E. Bach,
the contented Kapellmeister's second son.

He plays Diatonic
then arpeggio ...
chords concord.

Brahms and Beethoven were desolate,
comforted by crotchets, quavers and minims.

Schumann lost will to live,
diseased, distressed and in disorder.

Distrait Mozart composed for exalted wind,
expired at thirty five, *The Requiem* unfinished.

Nietzsche and Wagner performed con animo,
perhaps Wagner suffered
low self-esteem as much as any.

I, the flying Dutchman,
hear cellos, violins and viola
convoke within.

Motets, aria and motif,
impassion as I transexist
on the ocean's movements.

Schoenberg's twelve tone music
piqued the Nazis;

Orchestras played for Nazi officers
in voluptuous quarters,
Music, murder and Teutonic atrocity.

The High Gate and gravel paths
lead to odious barracks
where prisoners hanged from the rafters.
Human smoke from crematorium
billowing in wind; effluvium.

The boat pulls out.
I (The Flying Dutchman) repine.

For twenty seven years I've wandered seas
solicitous for Senta's love

that may reprieve
and repose me again.

'Requiem aeternam dona eis, Domine.
Libera me,' is sung.

Miserere nobis
Dona nobis pacem. After Bach.

LUX AETERNA.
MAHLER'S 'AUFERSTEHEN'.

Daniel O Connell at Tara

for Desmond O Grady

Thirteen hundred vehicles roll
from Dublin
towns in green and white.
A mist – a sea of banners –
descends on Tara.
Forty bands march,
ten thousand horsemen,
multitude countless
as the bearded grain.
I parade on horseback
apparelled in my green uniform
and green repeal cap,
horsemen to my left and right.
The sound of mass is on the wind.
I speak with the gale,
give a stirring repeal oratory.
Afterwards I, Daniel O Connell,
partook of tea, yellow meal bread
and herrings
in Maguire's teahouse.

Parnell to Queenie

from Ó Pharnell go Queenie by P Ó Snodaigh
for Noreen Walshe and Gerry Harte

Poem 11

I don't want to be without you
That's true, a fact
They can say that there was a
time when I didn't know of your existence.
True too ....
But now
I know and I don't wish the opposite,
your absence.

I am there for you, woman
I am
There for you, woman.
I am.

My love,
magpie you are,
take this kiss on the back of your talon
take it with you
to the nest of memories

and may it
glisten for you
by day and always.

Maximus

for Michael Herlihy, Máire Hearty, Conor Brosnan

She danced and gyrated all
night, in her negligee.

Whiteheaded, bashful,
ectomorph and *épatante*.

Her ego-thought deranged,
a stale and living pseudo-corpse.

She cocks the revolver
to her cranium.

She has lost all. She is
almost beyond Hope.

Mauvaise heure past,
Again *compos mentis*,

she repeats to herself
and everybody,

'I love you all,
whom I forgive.'

She roars,
'*Maximus*'.

Everybody

for Peter Dunphy

Alone on the old sheep track,
the wind blowing
against cynical *Homo Erectus* –
Bearded, tall,
slim and rancorous.
To maybe walk for hours.
No laws, no judgements,
neither good nor bad.
Alone in the pattern
of electrons whirling
around in an unknown hemisphere.
He commences to live on,
to lose all
in his dysteleology,
float in fugue,
shout on Conor Hill.
What is the wind?
To sit on stone,
scrape his body against turf,
sink in the soggy soil.
He is an alien who must
acknowledge alienation.
'Despite the growth of
six thousand million years,
what is love, my father?'
'Homo Lacrimosus.
Everybody. Everything.'

Sceilig

for Con Moriarty

Stone splinter soul
of Michael.

Fulmar-filled theatre boxes
at Blindman's Cove.

Six hundred and seventy steps – we ascend
by Christ's saddle to six mortal cells.

Bells call to Matins
and Nones.

Norse abduct Eitgall
from Sceilig Mór.

Blathmac incanted: 'Glory of the screaming gannet
equals and surpasses the inchoate monks at prayer.'

The Monks' graveyard where stands the Priests' Stone,
Puffin sanctuary of Solitude and Sublimation.

Centuries later, morse code tickle
taps on the giant transatlantic cable.

All is almost silent,
the tourist boats chug.

Two jets powerline
overhead to America.

Mist lifts. Lights of God
shine with atonement.

IV

Muhammad Seid

I
I, Muhammad Seid,
have lost my parents,
my other children and
my wife.

They endured as much
as is possible.
Privation
is total.

I cry as Abdu, my beautiful son,
and Marema, my comely daughter,
arrive, in fever,
to a *Forenge* Camp.

Forenges do their best;
force feed them
with *waha* (milk) and *watet* (water).
Marema and Abdu are *in extremis*.

I wait, watch and touch Marema
and Abdu prostrate on the ground
amidst hundreds in delirium
in the typhus-tents.

At dawn my dear Abdu,
my dear, dear Marema
deceased –
are lifted from the camp

on bamboo leafed biers.
We dirge-dance
with our dead ones
to the mosque behind Harbo village.

Our forty precious ones,
bodies covered
in *abijede*
are interred in a mass grave.

II
After the flash floods
there is nothing left to offer
we straggle from the washed out
Forenge camp

– I failed to produce crops.
The drought left us nought to drink
and eat – I reflect – as I drift along
with ten thousand refugees.

Tall, thin, marasmic bodies
mix in shuffling groups,
their wood-bundles loaded on donkeys,
trudge on the mud road.

Children caper along the road,
mothers feed babes.
Men drove animals.
Cachectic creatures implode.

Some children resemble Marema and Abdu.
I long for them and despair as dearly-
loved ones apart do. I myself know
the *agonia* of Allah's punishment.

III
At Adis-Mender
farm workers of the Party
are kind to us shocked
and inconsolable people.

Fifty truck loads of Wolloeans,
dressed in brown smocks
forced to travel south
for resettlement.

A Harbo villager
croons
consecratory hymns
to Allah;

Weakened by tribulation
and lamentation,
strained and disenabled
by grief.

There is Resignation
as the implacable and
shimmering sun bakes
from the Southern sky.

Famine has despoiled.
The Rains may fall.
We need to sow, wind and
reap with sickle again.

Adamh Agus Ádhamh

do Aogán ó Muircheartaigh agus Pádraig ó Snodaigh

Thit buama eithneach ar an ndomhan
agus lean deich míle roicéad é.
Faic fágtha.

An pléascadh nuicléach,
lean na stoirmeacha tintrí,
básanna raidiam, an geimhreadh eithneach.
Róstáladh nó reodh cách.

Níl corr éisc ag siúl ar thrá,
ná faoileán ag seilg bídh
ar chladach, ná lacha ag snámh
ar dhromchla an uisce.

Níl leanaí ag siúl ar scoil,
ná ag imirt peile,
ná ag rith de shíor.

An t-adamh
tá eolas air.
Ádhamh agus Éabha
chuir eolas ar an úll.

Óm chroí amach
bhfuil tarrtháil ann
ó scoilt an adaimh
agus Ádhamh ionainn?

Atom and Adam

from Adamh agus Ádhamh
for Catherine Christie, Caoimhe and Family

A nuclear missile discharged.
Ten thousand rockets
fired and fissioned.

Firestorms flared, radiation
deaths from global
fallout, Nuclear Winter
gripped Mammalia.

The heron stands no more,
no seagulls hunt for sprat
nor whistling drakes
transmigrate the seas.

No children walk nor run
to school, nor disport;
Pompeiian.

Can we be salvaged
from knowledge of the quasar
and quark, Eve and Adam's
Apple of Discord?

We have filled the seas
with our Song,
Peroration
and Tears.

V

Cathal

in memory of Cathal Stritch
for the 1977 U.C.D. Medical class &
for Patricia Fitzsimmons and the Sligo team who organised the reunion

The tree blossomed in full,
a balloon in the sky. He ploughed
long fields, set seed in *Terra Firma*.

He weeded onions that grew in long
brown drills. The Co-Op repositories
were full. He was composed.

To build a new house, that was his
responsibility or respite. Rocky
Mountain gales gusted and reposed.

Then the Great Abruption:
Requiest in Pacem.
Cathal sailed home.

Tonight or Tomorrow

This mephitic cancer has seeped,
rebound all my body,
into every cell,
I must give up this insane
and peculiar fight.
I dread that I will fight no more.
So the denigration recurs;
I may die tonight or tomorrow.

Misere mei, Deus.
So what is to be, must,
as this marauding cancer,
has robbed me of my reasons
for existence. These pleasures
and possessions, I will
certainly miss. I denounce
myself. I discompose my children.

Does life commence for me
after death,
as in Valley of the Kings,
where Ra might pass increscent,
each night?
But Terracotta guards
will not protect me,
as Lord of Qin.
I will not be a Homer,
a Sophocles,
a Hesse nor a Christ.
The Black Death has visited me.

I misprized this cough
that chokes me,
but I cannot flee
and write my Decameron.
I die a Dante in exile,
my Beatrices
damned *in perpetuum*.

I am in an incorporeal city,
as this radium has drained
and impugned me.
I am too weak
to turn in bed.
I care not to live or die
as I leave behind
my twisted and tarnished body
on earth,
and pout final contrition
and testament.

May God have compassion
on me, I perhaps,
should as Michelangelo,
sing to God,
as God may take
or leave me,
pro tempore.
The choice is not mine.
I remise my soul
and am exonerated
in my opiate respite
and *Refugium*.

Father

for my mother

Craak craak call of corncrake,
cuckoo's opulent song
and exuberant pigeon hooting
transmuted throughout the sea, sand
sound-scape of Castlegregory.

Meticulous you were,
and weeded vegetables
running in multilinear rows
time and time again
in Farrell's ghost-
breathing garden.

Mick, member no. 8600,
Blue tunic, uniformed,
sitting self-realised
and steadfast
in the ochre-walled
station-office
of brown linoed floors,
S.O. books and wall maps.
You, petulant and prudent
amongst your tuniced colleagues
and merciful souls.

Síocháin's Spiorad Dé ar d'anam
Míle céad míle buíochas duit, m'athar.

The photographs blur,
O gentle and beloved father.

Kieran

My beloved brother
Kieran's mission is complete.

I am overcome
at this wanton loss.

Good man, good soul,
faithful brother, healer.

I stare into the soul of death
stare and must also face the anguish.

May your soul rest this evening
for ever in the midst of angels everywhere.

Nature's violence: the white
waves crash and lash coasts.

I am mortal and wounded
by your loss.

Your cross ... as sad as His,
Grief everywhere. Loss.

I witness for you this night
of your death, brother.

Recall the long, relentless ... Kieran, what is it
that you say? ... Football, fun-filled.

Long, relentless, football
fun-filled

give me these carefree words,
not a word of incomprehensible grief,

just for a moment,
... 'fields'.

Long, relentless, football fun-filled,
fields of Camp and Castlegregory.

Then your profession where you cared
with gentle hands for thirteen years.

For your soul was all good, expansive,
total exemplar, in such time,

Before Sorrow struck,
met you, stripped you.

The clock strikes Three,
twelve hours dead.

Ciarán of Clonmacnoise, the Apostles,
Christ and Mary repose with you.

VI

Almost Pink

(Cahir IV)

Almost pink sky,
after five and twenty years;
return to Cahir refuge.

The tidal river circuits cows' mandibles
transparent in water bed.
Minnow takes first leap.
Shoal of mullet sliver up stream.

Cloud shadows thrown
on the purling river,
the bank marsh,
the rushes grey green and singed
after black winter's snap.

Still lark trills in evening sonata,
three human voices respond
– essentially in this fugue
all, even love leads to departure.
This evening she photographs
into the lime-white, yellow sun.

The lark soars, melodises as always,
wings beat,
descends to marsh
to recommence the ritual of revival.
The movement ends.

Thrush development amongst goldheavy,
yellow furze, coppices in perimeter
below run of dusk blue mountain.

Cahir river rounds to ice blue sea,
the tide marks sand-dunes;
sandhoppers, as tide retraces,
reclaim inch by inch.

Journey since we left you
five and twenty years ago
– canto of love and requiem;
you repose us by the lake,
at the back, the sounds
of sea's percussion.

Water birds whistle all-night,
the swan stirs.
We were lucky then,
some are taken from this harsh planet
to heal in innumerable galaxies.

Three souls stride into the village.
Friends in this wayward world
of sacrifice.
Domine, sustain us
in our calamities, dependencies.
Direct our course as stars
in the night sky exposition,
pulses of light ascending
into fragile songs,
sun's bells chant.

Body Points

That he would return to comforting sea.
Love, laughter, loss. Save, lose soul
of Fortune. *Om*. Regain the wind.
Call uncluttered song of soul again.

He reclaimed flesh and blood, touched
Love's Body Points of mind and soul
in gold and yellow stone house of lilies
past, present, future faces and forms.

Six and sixty immutable swans atone on Lough Geal,
the swallows swish south west of lake.
Thrush and Blackbird record – Listen to men's, women's
seven rainbow voices – Fast. Care. Sing. Wait.

The blue horseman gallops the cobalt sky
Round his neck flowers as yellow.
Bold red colours he wears in fateful Passage
covered in saffron oils and the songs of Destiny.

Soul-Forces

I
Cerulean blue
envelopes,
evening is transposed.

Still ribbon lakes,
Pedlar's coum nested;
beyond oxbow lake forming.

Mountain's mosaic, five hundred million
years of rock, built up
on Iapetus, Palaeozoic ocean.

Raw umber mountains
levelled mesozoic, reformed,
the waterfall outflows.

Seas over and beyond
flow in and out of the channel
circuit.

What is all this intimacy
shared in this planet
of everlasting change?

Cars in convoy
over bronze age terrain
lost in admiration –

The butterflies on edge
of beechwoods.
Waves fall on shorelines.

All love moves
sculpted in fossils
along flow of river.

Man stretches on ditch
at cross-roads, observes
evening's passengers.

II
Rembrandt

Precambrian farmer, silver
man, long grey coated,
damp-brown laced shoes

tramps road, climbs
townland possessed of Saskia,
ruby woman of scarlet world.

Oldman face of smiling memories
trudges into indigo night,
everywhere recalls.

III
Titian

Sacred love for her
splinters the orange sky

fractures steel
core of the world.

Titian shall not kiss her for fear
of deluge of tears profane torrent

nor procreate other child who
would publish an eirenicon.

IV
Tintoretto

Giotto painted wet
Paduan plaster.

Brunelleschi's perspective
of lightness and grace

Greek – El greco
beyond forms.

Love happiest, Botticellian
harmony attained.

Tintoretto's utterances:
And I miss thee loved one
and know better than anyone
souls shall be free.

After the sweetkiss,
the tender embrace,
the lilac body touches

Bless me as I blessed you
within rainbows.

Most intimate soul wide, broad
and deep ever touched.

Knowledge of love rouses contentment,
being, consciousness, bliss.

You are me; hear
supplication – that you
may sleep on my chest.

Curl upon me so perfect.
The birds whistle at dawn,
the wind sweeps from west.

Hear the exhortation, that
you heave, my soul-sea.

Always so calm,
such a fine time,
souls in safe dock.

At dawn two souls
trail out the Adriatic pelagos.

Princess,
Darling, Precious.

Thousands of loved ones
dance on the shore.

Thousands of her soul forms
career the heavens over Venice.

V
Titanium white butterfly
flies low over ultramarine sea,

risks drowning
from waves,

self assured, patterns
to former, present, future soul-friends,

then flaps to lapis lazuli butterfly
in bed of birds foot trefoil.

The seven souls
rise, criss-cross

soar over viridian field,
wing over dazzling dunes.

Love, Shame and Rage in Yugoslavia

I cannot reach you.
Snow has fallen .... White canvases.
But in this nuclear winter
 our ordnance drivers still brazen
the crunching ice.
But I cannot meet you
in this compromised war zone.

There is little point to discurse
in this flash point of history.
My word is ad hoc. The snow drifts
have slowed the movements of our front lines.

I know that you slept – rats skulked overhead
and our love surely mortified. I shouldn't even
be happy to see you.

Ironically on the Feast of The Epiphany
I bring you gifts of nothingness, despair
mortal love, shame and rage.
Thankfully you have nothing for me.

Rays of sunlight beam through on the ice-
swollen lake and snow garmented fields.
Distasteful smiles light up faces
as we sense a doomed spring offensive,
fallout and unconditional surrender.

VII

Verbum et Verbum

This section contains twenty-six poems
composed to selected folios from the Book of Kells.
The folios are indicated with each title.
Variations on stanza forms are used.

Introduco

Cuckoo's call-song
blends in polylight
from dawn day-long.

Colm Cill's delight,
monks alone,
swallows' flight.

Monk's None
pursuit of sanctity,
thrush intone.

Study scripture in humility,
fast in oratorium,
labour in mill in servility.

In solemn *monasterium*
the tuniced grey-monk strokes,
barefoot in scriptorium.

Canon Tables

F 2v

Halo with three
crosses under arc.

Plates cross-referenced
to Mathew, Luke, Mark.

Evangelist, God and author torn apart
by four Zoomorphic creatures' bark.

63

Mother

F 7v

With smile and pen
'soul is in a way
all things' within.

For Mary, Holy Angels may
with calf, lion, eagle and
Sacred Jesus for her pray.

Dress is the Sun regal,
the Moon under her feet,
stars ornament temple.

M

F 12r

Embellished *Breves Causae
and Argumenta* imbue.

Precious exegesis
not eisegesis, to ensure.

Monolith M
concealing Matthew.

Evangelists

F 27v

*Homo, Leo, Vitulus,
Aquila* gallop,
white, red, black,
pale horses. Hup!

Pay homage to lamb
of seven horns
and seven eyes –
spirits forlorn.

Images approach
illustrated on vellum.
Portraited, scripted
indivisible *verbum*.

St. Matthew

F 28v

St. Matthew, tax collector,
understood well and more –

fatuous men mistreat women who beget
love fools for a time, then regret.

St. Matthew you collected tax and rates
from fish-buyers, fishermen, advocates.

St. Matthew, may the eagles of concern
that circumcircle you allow to learn

repair disputes and terror,
not distract any longer.

God's calf, You realise not by chance
world's ironic ways and acceptance.

Encircle us from addictions,
yellow devils of Deceptions.

Protect us from the beast born
with seven heads and ten horns.

Liber Generations

From Abraham to David
fourteen generations
to the Babylonian exile
fourteen more nations

to Emmannuel's coming
fourteen sets of births –
Father's and Mother's
work, tears, deaths.

Anointed one, enlighten.
Dispense anodyne
to us, liberticides,
who tense and repine.

Portrait of Christ

White, red lead gleam,
orpiment, Lapis Lazuli
expensive ultramarine,

Folium, kermes vivify-
woad, verdigris
mixed with vinegar to dye

applied on vellum to decree
Christ illustrated on full page
– ornamented god's mystic Trinity.

Peacocks, chalice, vines engage,
vindicate, as do Fish, Snake,
Lion of God, comfort with age.

Eight Circle Cross

F33r

St Columba journeyed
well to Iona, Kells;
founder father of scripts
illuminated, comparable

to Alexandrian Chronicle,
St. Gall's texts, Lindisfarne,
Book of Durrow and Mac Regol
or Turin Gospel that warn.

Eight bequests of Holy spirit
Bless us eight times over
and over again with cross
of eight circles to sober!

Christ Autem Generatio

F34r

Geometrical, phyllomorphic spectre
figure representation letter-list.
Three angels with book and sceptre,

cats, rats, otters, fish persist.
Diamond, circles, squares, rectangles,
head impaled by Rho – transfixed,

Mice nibble Corpus Christi and mangle:
floral page with spiral, trumpet,
triquitera curved bands, knots dangle.

Soul of hand B, Designer of Carpet
art of interlacing eight lines –
in self-mortification and in debt,

lives to embellish autumnal times
with marine blue, purple, yellow
and scarlet calligraphic signs.

Christ's Arrest

F114r

Passive, Osirian
Christ
much at risk

surrounded by moist
hissing snakes,
snarling dogs, biased,

avaricious, mocking rakes,
jealous, villifying, corrupt,
murdering liars, fakes.

Soldiers arrest Him usurpt,
three persons in one Being
circumornate Him, incorrupt,

en route to our Redeeming,
his patterned passion,
expiation and Our Healing.

Scandal

F114v

To live in *Paradisus* paragon, in
body mortal we carry death's sin.
Immortal Christ, *tunc* is the day
to be scandalised and saved.

Gape wide upon your hearts within.
Bang, beat all life's cymbals' tin.
With Christ surround self to win.
You will be assaulted by the way
but to live in *Paradisus*.
You will be violated by ravens again.
Bereave not passions, lost lust's yen.
You require Order, Perfection's ray
and music that transposes gay
releases hates, affliction.
To live in *Paradisus*.

Spreadeagle

F124r

Two rabid beasts spew
latticed wrath across.

Fifteen billion behold
Ecce Homo on cross,

blaspheme, indebted but not
indignant at your Loss.

Scriptorium

F130r

In the rural *rath* ring
– One roomed building
rectangular, stone walls low,
steep roof, minute window,
lintel over door, scripts wrapped
suspended in satchels strapped.

Here in scriptorium I transcribe
St. Mark, with swan quill describe,
dipped in inkhorn, coloured
yellow purple, blue, red.
I stroke, graph
on skin of calf.

INITIUM engages me;
better than to be
milking fecund cows,
tending weak ewes,
milling oats in haste,
sweating in lime furnace!

It's fine for Mark
reposing on bark
of T grasped firmly by demented
dragons! I punctuate, ornament
spiral, interlacing and
patterned diaper band.

I am protected from bevy
of snakes muscular and many,
serpents' heads in lair,
with my rulers, setsquare,
compass complete,
and Paraclete.

Hora Tercia

F183r

Mark reclines in space,
cantet aula caelestium,
reading *Et Deus*
erat verbum.

Protect me from swooning
into serpentine fears,
barbarous distraction of
Palaeographer's peers.

Rectangles, squares,
diamonds, parchment,
waxed tablet, quills,
stylos, statement

of Himalayan blue
from lazuli lapis,
vermillion red – *ars
pulchra, vita brevis*.

Forasmuch – 781A.D.

From XRI ad DI
SEVENTY-SIX generations,
Quoniam has tested
the durable patience.

Year seven eighty-one
long morbid black winter,
a break from penning seventeen
lines to the page year after year.

Spiral and trumpet patterns
elaborate Quoniam
twenty elders
encased in *niam*.

Rectangles, semicircles,
diamonds circumscribe
multicentricities
of terminal lives.

Snedriaghal, Abbot Cluain Nic
Nois, Maelcombair, Abbot Sliabh
Dá Locha,
this year deceased

QUONIAM.
Forasmuch she and he sins.
Arcane scriptures embolden
against horses, griffins.

Squeak of lizards,
Foxes hunt,
low murmur of starlings, goats
bleats, hogs grunt

Bellum inter genus
783 anno.
Conaill et Eoghain.
Stags bellow.

Qui Fuit – 793A.D.

F200r

Thirty years old behold
He began His prophesy
He was Joseph's son bold –

genitor of integrity.
Abbot of Achadh-bo
expired in Germany.

Lex Comain promulgated all
throughout Connaught
in seven ninety-three's fall.

Black ink from soot,
brown ink from apple-oak,
fifty/fifty cut.

Green and yellow stroke
and a good dab of brown,
a third of each soak

on top of each other tone,
filius ioseph qui fuit Heli
seeds to dispel despair sown.

Qui Fuit

F100v

Who was the son of Mathath
iae progeny

(blunder).
Great wind blew,
lightening and thunder
blasted this year.
Reachrainn plunder.

Showers of blood pour
as might have done
when pharaohs roar;
entombed Moses
at Bethpeor.

Bran, ardcheana.
Rex Laghinensi,
occisus est.
Gratias agimus tibi.

Tu Solus Sanctus – 802A.D.

F201r

Who was the son of Joram,
Joseph, Matthat, Jesse,
David,
certe.

Fine, abbess of Cilldara
perished.
'*Cellachaidh cum oratorio*
novo ardescit.'

Church of Colm Cille
despoiled for booty.
Number put to sword was
eight and sixty.

Still we carry on great
work on vellum-vita;
calf skin immersed in lime
cleansed with luna.

Qui sedes ad dextram
Patris misere nobis
in terra inferna.
Dominus cum vobis.

Credo

Nahson, Amminadab, Jacob, Isaac,
Abraham – believed
*IN UNUM DEUM, NUNC, TOTUS MEUM
ET POPULUM* – were relieved.

Numerous churches
razed to ground.
Two hundred calves slaughtered.
Plunder, war and famine abound.

Quill shakes. St. Cianan for us
under interdict we beseech.
Patricius, Colmcill,
Columbanus to God intercede.

Qui Fuit Di

Cakes converted into blood.
With human voice birds uttered in jest.
Torbach, scribe, lector,
Ard-macha abbot laid to rest.

Later Tuathal
wise-man, scribe and guest
doctor of Cluain-mic-Nois
mortuus est.

QUI FUIT DI
who was best,
the son of God
INCARNATUS EST

CRUCIFIXUS
RESURREXIT
et terra sub Deo est,
eum non cognovit.

Temptation

F202v

In *monasterium*, I live in the cell
apart, and study Cathach well.

Pray, fast, study, work in the mill,
self-sustain, effect God's will.

Clonard's three thousand monks intone
Finnian's rule impose dictum's groan.

Left, to meet in Kildare chapel
fair woman, plucked Love's apple.

Live in expectation of the torment
the temptation that will not relent.

Pater meum, adveniat regnum tuum.
Pater, sanctificetur nomen tuum.

Holy Spirit

F203r

Embellished patterns interlacing
lines, rectangles, encircling

ornament *IHS AUTEM PLENUS*
Spiritu Sancto-Deus.

Adsum. My soul subsumed.
Dove of God exhumed.

Jesus Lives

Angels announce
to Magdalene, Mary –
Jesus rises, recounts.
Angels announce
on Una week-day – renounce,
be wary.
Angels announce
to Magdalene, Mary.

Fire burns within.
Repent and Love.
Turn from sin
Fire burns within.
Leviathian tests our skin.
Dragon spews on God's Dove.
Fire burns within.
Repent and Love.

Sing swift-winged angels
turquoise, blue and yellow.
Bong the bells,
Sing swift winged angels,
navigate us from hells
ad Terram Di – us below.
Sing swift winged angels –
turquoise, blue and yellow.

St. John

Inveighs
Nahum
Nineveh.

St. John hums, *Om*
'*AMA*.
Laudate Dominun.'

Tenere memoria –
Scribe's word on quill.
Apo ... calipsa.

Verbum

Lindisfarne *Verbum* rhyme
from Christ, Cross of God
palliates world's crime.

Embellished *verbum* on line –
end, circle, rectangle,
cross and half circle sign.

Initium of time, *om*
Calligraphy,
verbum et verbum.